WORK & DAYS

WORK & DAYS

poems

TESS TAYLOR

 RED HEN PRESS | PASADENA, CA

Book layout by Latina Vidolova

Library of Congress Cataloging-in-Publication Data

Names: Taylor, Tess.
Title: Work and days : poems / Tess Taylor.
Description: First edition. | Pasadena, CA : Red Hen Press, 2016.
Identifiers: LCCN 2015041755 | ISBN 1597097322 (pbk. : alk. paper)
Classification: LCC PS3620.A979 A6 2016 | DDC 811/.6—dc23
LC record available at http://lccn.loc.gov/2015041755

978-1-59709-732-1

The National Endowment for the Arts, the Los Angeles County Arts Commission, the Los Angeles Department of Cultural Affairs, the Dwight Stuart Youth Fund, the Pasadena Arts & Culture Commission and the City of Pasadena Cultural Affairs Division, Sony Pictures Entertainment, and Ahmanson Foundation partially support Red Hen Press.

First Edition
Published by Red Hen Press
www.redhen.org

ACKNOWLEDGMENTS

Thanks to editors at *Academy of American Poets, Alaska Quarterly Review, Blackbird, Colorado Review, The Common Online, Harvard Review Online, Hudson Review, Guernica, Literary Hub, Poecology, A Poetry Congeries,* and *Tabula Poetica,* where some of these poems appeared—sometimes in different forms. The poem "Apocalypto w/ Radio" appeared in the anthology *99 Poems for the 99 Percent.* Many thanks to Dean Rader for making this possible, and also for generously sharing Hesiod with me. The poem "Time on Earth" appeared as part of an online project called *Poets for Living Waters* designed to support healthy oceans and rivers.

Thanks to the MacDowell Colony, the Headlands Center for the Arts, and the Berkshire Taconic Community Foundation for gifts of time to write.

Thanks to Amy Clampitt for the love and scrupulous care she brought to the act of watching the world and for the house and time she so generously left to writers.

Thanks to Mary Jo Salter, Karen Chase, and Ann Close for guarding and tending to Amy Clampitt's legacy.

Thanks to Maeve O'Dea for connecting me with Farm Girl Farm and for a thousand other small kindnesses.

Thanks to Laura Meister and the whole farm crew for the gift of a year planting and harvesting.

Thanks to Dominic Palumbo for friendship and lessons in chickens and livestock.

Thanks to Heather MacDonald and Anuj Shah, and to James and Rebecca Wood for being community.

Thanks to Alice Quinn, Martha Collins, Camille Dungy, Aimee Phan, Valerie Miner, Kate Brady, Rosanna Warren, Edan Lepucki, David Roderick, Bonnie Costello, and Elizabeth Bradfield for friendship and close reading.

Thanks to Kate, Mark, Alisa, Selena, Alexa, and Tobi, for working to build an ecosystem for poetry.

Thanks to my family: Alice, Charles, Terry, Nancy, Taylor, Bennett, and Emeline—for filling the days, and for making the work possible.

To Taylor, as always, all my love.

for Jasmine and Caitlin

Contents

Hung with Snow 15

I

Peck Small Tracks 19

Stockbridge 20

Disquisitive 21

Mid-March 22

Beside the Thaw 23

Mud Season 24

Apocalypto w/ Birds 25

Time on Earth 26

II

Equinox 31

Field Report: April 32

Hardening Off 35

Elsewhere Flood 36

May Day 38

Field Report: June 39

III

Method 43

Solstice (Lake) 44

Four Summers 45

High July 46

Soil Black. 47

Apocalypto for a Small Planet 48

Bright Tide 50

IV

In Late Summer 55

Punctuations. 56

With Vetch 58

Apple Buttering 59

Three Gleanings 60

Harvest Fair 63

Last Hay 64

After Freeze. 65

To Be Led Home 66

Apocalypto w/ Radio. 67

Field Report: December 69

Solstice (Eclipse) 70

Epilogue. 71

But why linger? Why stay in this world of oak and tree and rock?

—Hesiod, *Theogony*

HUNG WITH SNOW

Housman was right:

your life is short.
To miss even this springtime
would be an error.

I

PECK SMALL TRACKS

Novitiate to the winter's glaze
by day you weave your songs in white.

Then dusk falls, rich Madonna blue.
Branches shuttle icy rosaries.

Lights flare, swim the evening black.
The page waits. Again you try

to print a common thing: how this one day
slipped by—at dawn shadows bloomed

then shrank by noon to pinnacles.
Outside: the tree's dark alphabet.

After rain, the field, a pockmarked carpet.
Beneath the ice some seed

holds code, waiting warmth to speak it.
Now the night is ink, the field is wide:

you look to peck small tracks across it.

STOCKBRIDGE

From Wisconsin before it was Wisconsin
a glacier hauled these stones you stand on.

They traveled on its rubble.

They are the glacier's spit, its fissured teeth,
the path it garbled on its travel.

In 1880, the Stockbridge, last of the Mohicans,
were removed to Wisconsin: white edict

impassive as a glacier.
This town and farm and gabled houses

all are built upon that absence.
Now you bend into this field to clear it.

        You think of a frozen fist,
of ice-sheets melting. Glaciers lost

in too-warm early weather.
The west wind blows in from Wisconsin.

Each stone you touch is cold as bone.
As if it holds some trace of spirit.

DISQUISITIVE

Alone in the village, in the heart of winter,
you read John Clare in an old lady's cottage.
There are filigreed notes in your book's margins,

doilies in odd drawers.
In the town's main café,
students huddle by woodstoves.

Farmers read catalogs, order seed packages.
You drive icy roads between chapped farmhouses.
Valentines glitter in village windows.

You shovel snow, hike to get groceries:
run by the horse-barn, climb the town mountain.
Your husband comes up on the weekends.

You try to dislodge faulty friendship, miscarriage:
in the distance, war drones.
Our country murders somebody's children.

You read field guides, welcome few visitors.
Prepare to work one farm for a season.
Your economy is your life as a watcher.

You think:
you have been given time.
You hear it tick.

O says the clock:

You have. Given time.

MID-MARCH

Watching a floe
slide from a precipice
over the waterfall out of the ice-pond

is like watching obsidian.
Glass at a million degrees—
But we touch it, it dents, fluid cold.

Now in the gorges
the last ice-skulls. Cold trolls
the hills even as

frozen lakes grow cloudy
& open—
but to look at what? This thorny

landscape's bony
as November. All melt reveals
is half-rotten souls:

husks, garbage the snow hid.
Wrappers choke marshes.
Water, you move,

but you feel black as stillness.

BESIDE THE THAW

We bow into the rows that winter tore.
March tenders this warm day.
Our shovels grunt inside the mulch.

We tamp down muddy beds, lay burlap paths,
prod bodies out of winter slumber.
Pile fieldstones by the spring.

Work: one row to clean and then another.
Unearthing rocks is like dislodging anger.
We break and sit along the ragged grassline.

Eat beside the thawing river.
Our backs too are small stones in the sun.

Mud Season

We unstave the winter's tangle.
Sad tomatoes, sullen sky.

We unplay the summer's blight.
Rotted on the vine, black fruit

swings free of the strings that bound it.
In the compost, ghost melon; in the fields,

grotesque extruded peppers.
We prod half-thawed mucky things.

In the sky, starlings eddying.
Tomorrow, snow again, old silence.

Today, the creaking icy puller.
Last night I woke

to wild unfrozen prattle.
Rain on the roof—a foreign liquid tongue.

Apocalypto w/ Birds

the CUCKOO
is dying out all over England
loud old senior, LAUDE SINGE

what
summer is a common
Summer is a coming
is Icumen

how?

When they are gone will we cry
like the owl

who

Time on Earth

i

New to country stars, you try
to identify the constellations.
Cassiopeia, Andromeda—

You half forget their stories.
But on warming nights you see them
& your throat fills with hymns,

some ancestral body's holdfast tunes
to which your words are also blurred or blurring.

ii

You read about Physologus,
Greek cosmologist; mythic namer of the universe.
You borrow Amy's Audubon

& wander trying to match
shoots in mulch
to names. Embryonic skunk cabbage,

jack-in-the-pulpit,
maple spangling the forest air—
You dream an orrery of leaves and bones.

You say: *tow-hee* and *cali-cut,*
and walk repeating names you've gathered
just to feel their pleasure on your tongue.

You call *earthstar, club moss,* and *vibernum.*

iii

Beyond this, the constellated light-map.
Oildrums, tankers, spirochetes,

terrorists, radios, specimens,
ice cream, methamphetamine,

pandemics, global economic crisis.
Then you burn the paper, watch its turquoise flame.

This is not always, but you think

This is my time on earth.

Today a thumb-sized frog
clambered up the screen.

                                   Underbelly
shaking, skin grappling

all elements, a scrambling borderland,
a moving porous country.

Watching, you forgot to feel alone.
Delightedly, you called

A frog! A frog! out to the rustling woods.
And that was all. O wriggler.

With your sudden hope you also
sang your own short springtime song.

II

Equinox

Manure. This season's geese.
Out of marsh beds, Joe-Pye squeak.

Days parade the spring's assignments:
epic robin. Crocus. Sly chipmunk.

Rich, the neighbor's farmhand
(he learned to raise his ox by video)

harnesses the steers he got for free
and leads them out to clear a field,

to haul a fallen cherry out of mud.
He says he's learning something people always knew

because it's better for the land:
his beasts are amiable and slow—

also insolent, unpracticed at the yoke.
They nudge each other crookedly:

He goads them but they balk
forgetting how to turn or even walk.

All morning I watch as he cajoles them
in and out of swampy hollows.

They march the pasture, circling.
In raw wind they cut a furrow—

a line between the winter and the spring.

FIELD REPORT: APRIL

Quid faciat laetes segetes, quo sidere terram vetere . . .

"What must be done to bring a heavy harvest,
  under which stars to turn the earth . . ."
—Virgil, *Georgics I*

i

Mulching garlic: muck is heavy.
Everything is brown or gray.

Moving grasses, haying sprouts:
cold knobs rise, ache in my fingers.

ii

In this field not Pyrrah's bones or Deucalion's
but human remains:

no war
              (though even here farmers dig up old weapons)—

no helmets,
though while we work, the radio

broadcasts poppy harvests and bombings,
limbs shattering in another country—

In our field today:
              a lost child's sunglasses.

iii

Hot. Cold. Then a too-warm spell:
navies of clouds come and go, come and go—

windstorms, birds
                                    —all north too soon.

In the greenhouse
we plant nightshades,

tomatoes & cucumbers:
stage summer plenty while

the radio announces
dead seals in Labrador—

and above us rose-throated grosbeak return
from Tulum, from Oaxaca, those borderless migrants.

iv

Across the hemisphere, farmers start the old art.
Bow into broccoli.

Push machines or their bodies.
Plant starts or seed.

Buy oil for tractors. Cross borders. Spray pesticides.
Virgil wrote *by which signs shall we know?*

We too are small against great constellations.
We plant when the sun shines. We augur & pray.

HARDENING OFF

Blond mornings stretch,
naked sugar flashes. In the trees,
a hundred shades of micro-green

refract tipping frequencies,
chlorophyll in bright chartreuses.
In the greenhouse,

      lettuces we've coddled,
kale that's germinating
purplish gold—our speckled trout

(o tender leggy phloem) explode out—
sporting cracked seed husks, toppled helmets.
We turn off piped-in electric heat.

We march them out to line the open dirt.
They wait in flats outside all morning.
Cash crop. Green army.

We entrust them to the season.
Weather them & set to digging.
Kneel & copy what the trees

are even now above us doing—
coax the sugar out of light.
Turn the light into the feast of leaving.

ELSEWHERE FLOOD

i

No sooner begun than it goes wrong:
cucumber seedlings frozen on the stalk. Bok
choy full of beetles. Failures gnaw the crop.

Borrowed tractor, borrowed harrow, cleaning.
Money for replanting. Spreading traps.
Last year's debt a ditch to dig out of.

ii

Elsewhere famine, elsewhere flood.
Rainforest clear-cut for pasture.

Invasive beetles in the orange groves.
A pregnant woman inhaling sprayed poison.

iii

In the greenhouse: kale, more kale.
Outside: weather variable.
Sky's ADD, says Mora as we move

eggplant sprouts from 64s to 32s
shoving root hairs down, transplanting—
like copying notes out from a notebook,

doing rote-work, piece-work, on for hours—
tomatoes have a better survival rate than poems, I say,
and Mora laughs. Today

we move cukes and zukes with funny names—
cash crops for fancy restaurants—
things some patron will consume

in consommé, in heirloom salad.
For a moment, we're in the hopeful season.
Each name is sugar

we can sell: *Snowgold, Zebra, Green Dragon.*

May Day

They go, the early flags, the gory maples—
so too the daffodils & Lenten roses.
Other petals swirl & nights warm.

Buds thicken & cast shadows:
in a thunderstorm
I almost forget the ice that was.

Narcissi suckle watery paths;
meadows heap up emerald masses.
How green & I want to delight

except this undertow—it pulls so fast
passing before I recognize it.
Like souls in Dante who can't see the present,

white lilacs curdle in pre-summer heat.
The parade I barely noticed was beginning
is already halfway down the street.

FIELD REPORT: JUNE

A thousand leeks to plant. A flat, a tray. A season
to get in the ground today.
Long since light: shadows inch away.

We're here at six, at seven.
The tarp we work was meant to stave off weeds—
everywhere the weeds push in.

For hours we shove leeky handfuls,
hardened off for weeks. The air
is onion. For hours we crawl—heat

rides my back
like I'm its horse. I punch again,
stuff six to a row & on

all morning. Move by inches. Plant.
Try to find a rhythm as I go.
What cool there was has gone, has gone.

Dirt and weeds and greens and starts.
Tiny vales of shade retreat.
The long field of summer has begun.

III

METHOD

In the dirt you dig fragments.
Turn them and ponder.

Weed chard. Forms
morph like clouds.

At lunch, you write down
how in this jungle

a gem-backed toad startled
and hopped away—

how tiger lilies trumpet the sun.
In the bean patch brown spiders,

egg sacs on their backs.
Toddling through shadows,

sturdy & wobbling, they are
fragile, pregnant as summer now is—

SOLSTICE (LAKE)

Once again today our patron star
whose ancient vista is the long view

turns, full brightness now and here.
We loll outdoors, sing, make fire.

We have no henge here but after
our swim, linger

by the pond. Dapples flicker
on the pine trunks by the water.

Buzz & hum & wing & song combine.
Light is monument to its own passing.

Frogs content themselves in bullish chirps,
hoopskirt blossoms

on thimbleberries fall, peeper toads
hop, lazy—

     Apex. A throaty world sings *ripen.*
The grove slips past the sun's long kiss.

We dress.
We head home in other starlight.

Our earthly time is sweetening from this.

FOUR SUMMERS

for J.H.

i *fruit*

Thorny abundance—
Obsidian berries
fall now by handfuls.

ii *bulb*

Spring's mulched garlic: now swan's-neck scapes.

In the high field, we plunder:
        snap, snap, snap, snap.

iii *leaf*

Four hours to weed just one kale row.
Impossible. Lunch break.

Five more to go.

iv *fruit*

Already time to plant for fall.
Who plants no pumpkin now will then have none.

Any gourd's a time machine.
All winter we will feed on light and soil.

High July

On vines eggplants wobble.
    Corn looms yardsticks high—

extruded zucchini
    obscene delicata

    split yellow melons

now food for flies

We watch—mere human perception—
    baffled again when did it happen

    everything humid
    this weedy   too-muchness

birds beat us to fruit
        peck it senseless

growth, growth
    the sky overwhelming

fields tilt past fullness
    —life sticky with death—

Soil Black

Overcast in the fields
           meticulous labor

to rip the unwanted
           haul weeds to the woods.

Wheelbarrows of waste.
               The baby I planted this year

was only tissue. The botched ovum
           did not grow, did not even sprout.

On the computer, its sac
           was empty, soil black.

I bow into absence.
               & yes I know

many women have harder labors
           strapped to the seasons

& to the children
           strapped to their backs—

Apocalypto for a Small Planet

i

& the radio reports how in 2050
farming Massachusetts will be like farming Georgia—
all's flux, no one can say what will grow in Georgia,

where maples will grow then or whose fine taps
will sap sugar from the cold in spring. Will we get syrup
from the boreal forest, peaches from Massachusetts?

ii

Drone strikes & opium poppies.
Oil spills & poisoned wells.
Drought zone. Famine. War zone.

iii

Artisanal, this

       intervention:

what gift

     this day.

iv

My inner cynic says
don't bother this is navel gazing

& my friend at Yale says my hunger
to be near zucchinis

will not save the planet from real hunger
except I remember in the film on gleaning

when the priest in his compassion says:
those who glean now out of spiritual hunger

also should be fed.

v

Ecosystem of yard or field or mind:

these cucumbers are more art than science,
more daydream

than global action (if we separate the two).
But digging now I feel an otherness—

life, a great inhuman freedom—
here I work a plot that also grounds—

Bright Tide

for N.C.

i

Among all the harvests
these are ones we make myth of—

heat loosening squash
spicing the dew as we rush to fill

the restaurant order—
haul our ripe crates.

Organic cash crop:
to market, to market.

ii

New worlds on the sky,
sungold solar systems.

Gold balls on the chain.
We map our hands in the scent of tomato.

iii

Lost ones sag. Lost ones break.
Birds peck. The ground oozes.

The unpicked fruit wavers.
We catch what we can.

iv

Basic: between stalks for hours
in binary motion—ripe/ not ripe,

not mental really not boring either
decisions of thumb & forefinger

forging attunement
between body & vine;

as if picking were all we were made for—
  plop plop in crates

                    in our upturned shirts.

v

I was in the field the day you called
to say you'd lose the baby.

How your sac was broken, and there was
no saving it, just the waiting.

I stood there, the whole day wrapped around me.
I stood there, crying, smelling vine.

vi

Another day of work. Another.

vii

All month I thought of you, of us, the women,
of all the trying to & breaking open.

Of the rainsplit ones, the ones that burst.

And of the smells of vine & harvest.
I wanted to give you tomatoes.

viii

Here, a life is many ripened.
Sprung, the seeded cells,
a fragile mix of luck and tending.

Warm furzed blur of dust & buzzing.
Tangle risen from the mud & marching.
Here we are not self but species

breaking as we bend & also fruiting
pressing onward in the long bright tide:
        yes it breaks & yes it also swells—

IV

In Late Summer

i

Wind on the lake, sun in the corn.
We swam in the pond as long as we could.
We save the rich blue on our inner eyes:

the apples make sugar of light.
Even so the sun comes up late.
Fare-thee-well says the light in the wood,

& starlings scatter off from the yarrow.

ii

Afternoons expand into silence.

A page turns
in the mind-sized room.

Light on the floor plays cello tones.

It is not coming back, what has gone.
A conceit, a conceit:

some war & apocalypse wait
held off—a bit—in the cricket's chirp—

Punctuations

i

in bed new wind
trails through leaves & darkness;

& our bones lean together
as if knowing—

                                                         but what?

I think *autumn's long horn.*

But how?

                                               (*All this blowing*—)

ii

Below indigo mountains, corn,
nubbly gold.

Five o'clock cool & the water choppy:
lake empty, only we splashing.

For a while I fall into my breathing,
seeing the horizon switch

above lake weed, no longer thinking
"fall is coming" "dusk is coming"—I am present

in my own stroke, stroke, stroke.

iii

Cold nights, wet mornings.
We pick what lasts through frost.
Haul crates between remnants.

Tomatillos totter. A finch rides the air.
In the field, new music:

          the absence of crickets.

With Vetch

Meadowsweet smell:
goldenrod, thistle,
jewelweed & yarrow, more we can't name.

Wet stems we move through
to dig garlic heads,
long stalks now bound

with vetch & clover.
Underground creatures, they come up blinking.
We waken vampires

we mulched in March.
We squelch them up kelpy,
odd shrunken heads—

No starts now, no green:
only old bundles—dying & dead.

Apple Buttering

Coring a neighbor's apples,
bruised ones he left in bags by the door,

(Note: *Use these if you can or toss them*)

we are already in the season for
provisioning, rendering at dusk.

We carve good flesh from the husk.

Surgeons digging body parts from graveyards
would pare the rotten and the botched—

we hack the battered whole for parts.

Each cheek is a brown semaphore: *rot, rot.*
Worms wind through. The rest stews in the pot.

The sterile jars now wait.

As we slice, the day hovers.
Soon it will not.

Three Gleanings

i

Green drains from the hills and leaves
undertow & umbered rainbow.

Morning furrows fill with mist.
Warm noons we still harvest melons.

Chasing sugars on the vine
tasting sweetness after sun or rain:

flavor is the artifact of light.

All this heat & mineral & juice a clue—
the mystery summer strewed in passing—

ii

October morning: grasshoppers on kale.
        Everywhere they're clumsy, heavy-kneed.

In the field they are a fable:
        poor grasshoppers who sang all summer!

Many there & real, their clumsy wobbles
        are a death-jig: Summer's end.

Their elaborate joints climb toughened leaves.

iii

Dusk & moon out—we unlatch
potato cages. Furred tubers clutch

their six-months perch.
Annus mirabilis—odd alchemy.

Mulch and time
made these blind sprouts potatoes.

Hoisted in our hands they are chill comets.
We marvel at their oblong bounty.

Inside we scrub and slice, prepare
a pan with oil.

On the counter, old roots eye us whitely.

Harvest Fair

Anthropomorphic gourds on the trencher.
Cold local pears.

Undeniable chill in the air.
       Red sweetness in fists & in clustered stars—

       Neo-hillbillies play.

       In line for the bathroom, farm people check iPhones.
       "It's just apple picking against the apocalypse."

On the grill, veal. On the board, tender cow.
On the roast pig's black nose, drugstore sunglasses.

       Later, fiddlers & bonfire.
       Boys toss on a scrap pallet.

       Light flares on our faces.
       Timeless, how a few couples slink off now—

          to savor each other in corn rows, in darkness.

LAST HAY

As we do it we know we're spreading the summer—
mowed bales we unroll,
vitamin grass to swaddle our plantings,

garlic seed wedged, dragon's teeth in chill soil.
Over this we tamp a cut meadow,
summer's green skirt, laid down to rot.

Raking in sunshine
the spreading is sweet:
spice, heat and honey,

the good lover's bed.
Later the smell peels off in the shower.
Cold scours the night.

In fields, the frosts glitter.

AFTER FREEZE

Wasn't it last week that all this ripened?
Above us, bare trees rattle koans.

Wearing gloves we shroud the chard
inside tough hoops of tenting mesh,

frail gesture before long cold intervenes.
Low sun glazes scattered melons.

Lost skulls, they rot after the freeze.
No one will harvest them.

In the shed I sort the garlic seed.
In the chill we say: *Goodbye, goodbye.*

A customer drives off. The darkness comes.

TO BE LED HOME

Upright pillars. Bubbling windows.
Red tulips: the altar after Thanksgiving.

Out the window, picaresque snow falls.
One stern girl in a bonnet.

The austere faithful sing
"When we've been here 10,000 years"—

though it's barely 250, we are so new—
and in odd imperfect tribute

to Jonathan Edwards, Congregational missionary
who settled this valley

to convert then-called savages
& for whom these granite mountains

provoked "inward sweetness"
someone's translated

the hymn into Choctaw:
(*no words in the old language Tagkhanic*)—

& we wait in the silence
to be led home:

uneasy, hungry, I bow my head—

Apocalypto w/ Radio

But on the day that scientists announce that this past summer
was the third warmest in recorded time,

the blizzard's gaining speed and time

as I trace the Pike into the mountains.
The DJ says "some global warming,"

& indeed, my hands are finally warming

as the radiator blows 80-degree-heat
on the windshield. Black ice is forming

there and also forming

on the road and trees and hills.
I want to be off this slick road—

(it is hard to fathom any road

beyond the road you're on, to think of summer
overheating this cold world, to imagine summer

from inside a mountain storm).

That this story of this blizzard is connected
to summer or to the carbon that's connected

to arctic melting on our injured planet

is difficult to grasp. This ice

is present tense; any warming story
grows distant, a story

instruments of barometry tell.

I am brittle, small inside a storm.
Within a tide of growing storms

I know that what I want to know is slippery

as slippery as this road is slippery.
I am driving headlong in the dark.

FIELD REPORT: DECEMBER

The curtain's closed. Summer's field:
weed break on a snowy side-road.

Toppled cornrows, stems
in ice. Nearby—traces, tracks

& paw prints (rabbit, deer, perhaps a fox).
I also pass, a pregnant animal,

tracing one clumsy path in snow.
Subtle flutter: nuthatch, passing.

Along the river, silence opens.
Ocher and sienna stone.

Under the ice, freed water
mutters a green rune.

Cold pastoral: ice bobs on a floe.

Solstice (Eclipse)

The papers said "once in a generation"

and that morning looking out on snow

we read how the full moon darkened,

and for an hour our earthly shadow

stretched bloodred across the plate-white moon.

Then it passed and the wide round moon

turned its lone eye on fields and silos.

We hadn't seen it, hadn't tried, had been asleep.

That miracle swam above our faces

possibly the moment that I dreamed

again of the new planet we had seen.

Once-in-a lifetime glimmer, the first gleam:

O the froggy kick of bright new legs—

O fresh swim in my dark ultrasound.

Epilogue

Hands, everywhere, now tending
farms large or small, plots well or poorer.

Tracts I'll never see, hands pulling
onions to market, washing greens in clean water.

Loading avocados.
Squatting, unpacking.

Breaking to eat some lunch from home.
         Dozing under a tree in a calm hour.

May your bodies stay fed and your birds sing.
May our bodies stay fed and our birds sing.

I once met a man from Jalisco home again
after ten years working the garlic in Gilroy.

I once watched men hammer a stage set for a play;
actor-lovers spoke from plywood perches.

     The world is a made thing. The world is a made thing.

May those who are hungry be fed.
May those who have food also hunger for justice.

We bow to the work:
same & not same—our scattered arts—

removing, removing the stones from our soil.

Biographical Note

Tess Taylor grew up in Berkeley, California, where she led youth garden programming at the Berkeley Youth Alternatives Community Garden and interned in the kitchen at Chez Panisse. In her twenties, she dropped out of Amherst College to become a translator and chef's assistant at L'Ecole Ritz Escoffier in Paris. An avid gardener and cook, she is also an acclaimed poet. Her chapbook *The Misremembered World* was selected by Eavan Boland and published by the Poetry Society of America. Her work has appeared in *The Atlantic, Boston Review, Harvard Review, The Times Literary Supplement,* and *The New Yorker. The San Francisco Chronicle* called her first book, *The Forage House,* "stunning" and it was a finalist for the Believer Poetry Award. Tess is currently the on air poetry reviewer for NPR's *All Things Considered,* and was most recently visiting professor of English and creative writing at Whittier College.